I0816329

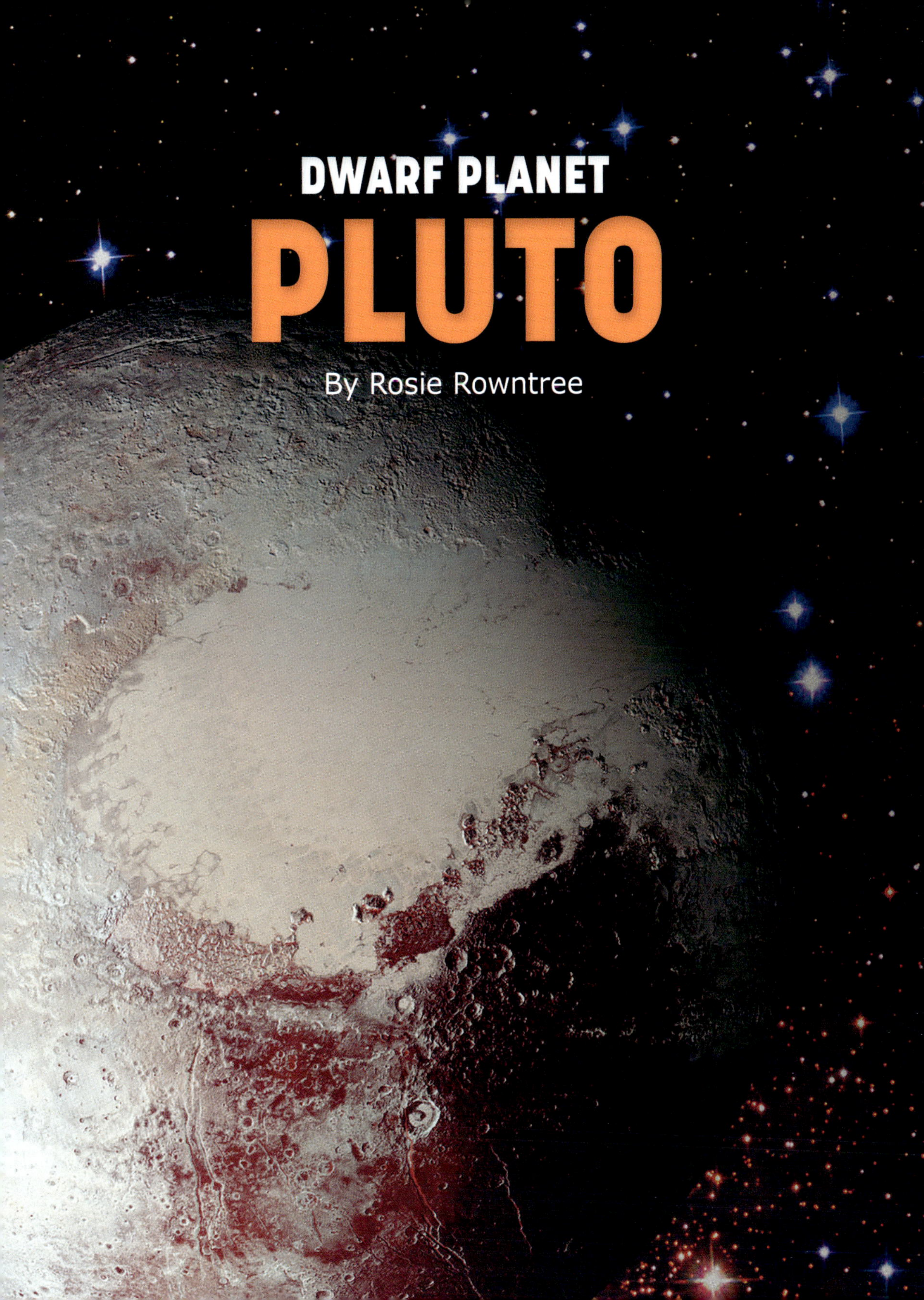

DWARF PLANET PLUTO

By Rosie Rowntree

CONTENTS

First published in 2026 by Hungry Tomato Ltd
F15, Old Bakery Studios, Blewetts Wharf, Malpas Road,
Truro, Cornwall, TR1 1QH, UK.

 A CIP catalog record for this book is available from the British Library.

ISBN 9781835696842

Manufactured in the USA

Discover more at
www.hungrytomato.com

Front cover image is an edited image of the New Horizons spacecraft and the dwarf planets Pluto, Ceres, and Haumea. Title page image is an edited image of Pluto. Contents page image is an edited image of Pluto.

Words in **BOLD** can be found in the glossary.

WHERE IS PLUTO?

Asteroid belt

Sun

Pluto is part of the **solar system.** Like the eight planets, it travels around the Sun. This journey is called Pluto's **orbit**. Pluto orbits the Sun once every 248 **Earth years**.

The time it takes a planet to spin around once is called a day. One day on Pluto is the same as 153 hours on Earth.

DWARF PLANETS

Pluto shares its orbit with many objects of a similar size – something that a planet shouldn't do. Because of this, scientists decided that Pluto should be called a "**dwarf planet**" instead.

Pluto is smaller than some of the solar system's **moons**, including Earth's own Moon!

Pluto isn't the only dwarf planet. Most dwarf planets, like Pluto, are in the **Kuiper Belt** beyond Neptune. One – called Ceres – is in the **asteroid belt** between Mars and Jupiter.

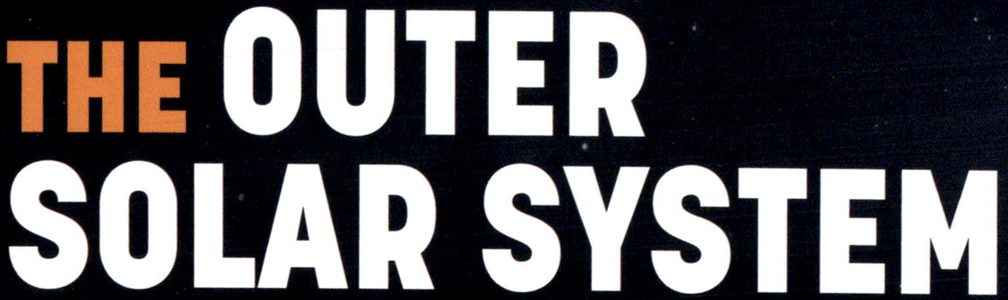

THE OUTER SOLAR SYSTEM

Before scientists discovered Pluto, people thought everything that traveled around the Sun had been found.

We now know that there are many small, icy objects far out in the solar system, beyond Neptune. This group of objects is the Kuiper Belt.

Scientists don't know exactly how many dwarf planets exist in the Kuiper Belt. There could be as many as 200! The four best known are Pluto, Eris, Haumea, and Makemake.

DWARF PLANET FACTS

Despite its small size, Pluto is a very surprising and complex world.

A kind of frost made from very cold **gases** covers the surface of Pluto. It also has a lot of **mountains**, valleys, and **plains**.

Pluto has a huge **glacier** made out of a gas called **nitrogen**. It's the largest glacier in the solar system and is shaped like a heart!

Pluto's orbit through space is shaped like an oval rather than a circle. Sometimes it's closer to the Sun than Neptune is!

WHAT'S THE WEATHER LIKE?

Because Pluto is so far from the Sun, it is a very cold place.

Pluto is tilted on its side a lot more than Earth is, meaning that its **seasons** are much more extreme than ours. Winter on Pluto lasts for **decades**!

The surface of Pluto is as cold as -385 °F (-232 °C)! This makes it even colder than Uranus, the coldest planet.

This is what scientists think the surface of Pluto might look like!

Charon, one of Pluto's moons

PLUTO'S MOONS

Even though Pluto is very small, it still has five moons. The largest, called Charon, is almost half the size of Pluto itself!

Scientists believe that Charon was created when Pluto crashed into something else in the Kuiper Belt, billions of years ago.

Pluto's surface is covered in frozen gases, but Charon's is made of water ice. It is possible that Charon had an ocean under its surface many millions of years ago!

THE KUIPER BELT

Scientists think there could be hundreds of millions of objects in the Kuiper Belt.

Most of these objects are very small and made mostly of ice. There are many more objects in the Kuiper Belt than there are in the asteroid belt.

Most of the Kuiper Belt is still unexplored – there could be hundreds of dwarf planets waiting to be discovered!

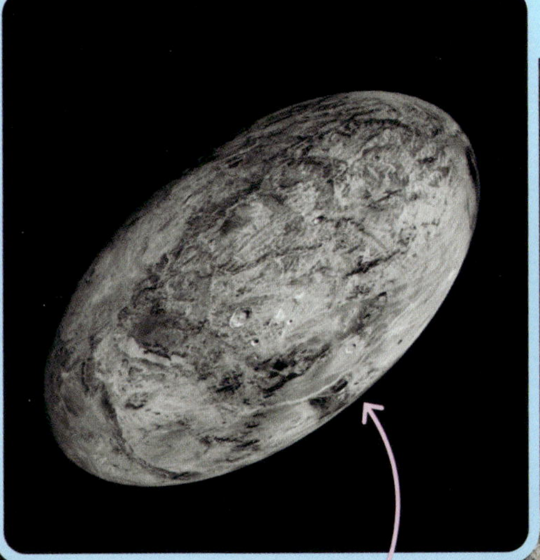

The dwarf planet Haumea is shaped like an egg!

It takes 557 Earth years for Eris to orbit the Sun!

WHAT CAN WE SEE?

Objects in the Kuiper Belt, including Pluto, are too far away to be able to take clear photographs from Earth.

Even the powerful **Hubble Space Telescope**, which is in orbit around Earth, finds it difficult!

Pluto's largest moon, Charon

Photo of Pluto taken by the Hubble Space Telescope

An **observatory** in Chile took photographs of Pluto and its moon Charon. These were used to help scientists who were working on a mission called New Horizons learn about Pluto's orbit through space.

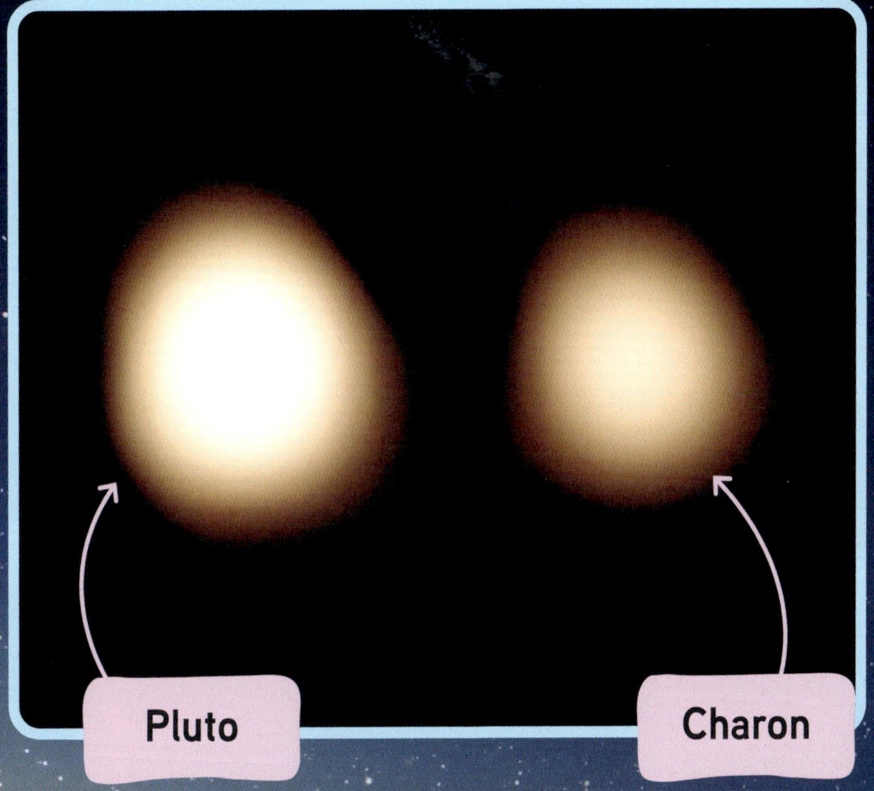

EXPLORING THE KUIPER BELT

New Horizons is the only spacecraft that has reached Pluto and the Kuiper Belt! It was able to take photographs of Pluto up close.

It took New Horizons nearly ten years to travel the huge distance between Earth and Pluto.

When it finally arrived, it helped scientists work out Pluto's true size for the first time!

New Horizons also studied Pluto's moons and several other objects in the Kuiper Belt.

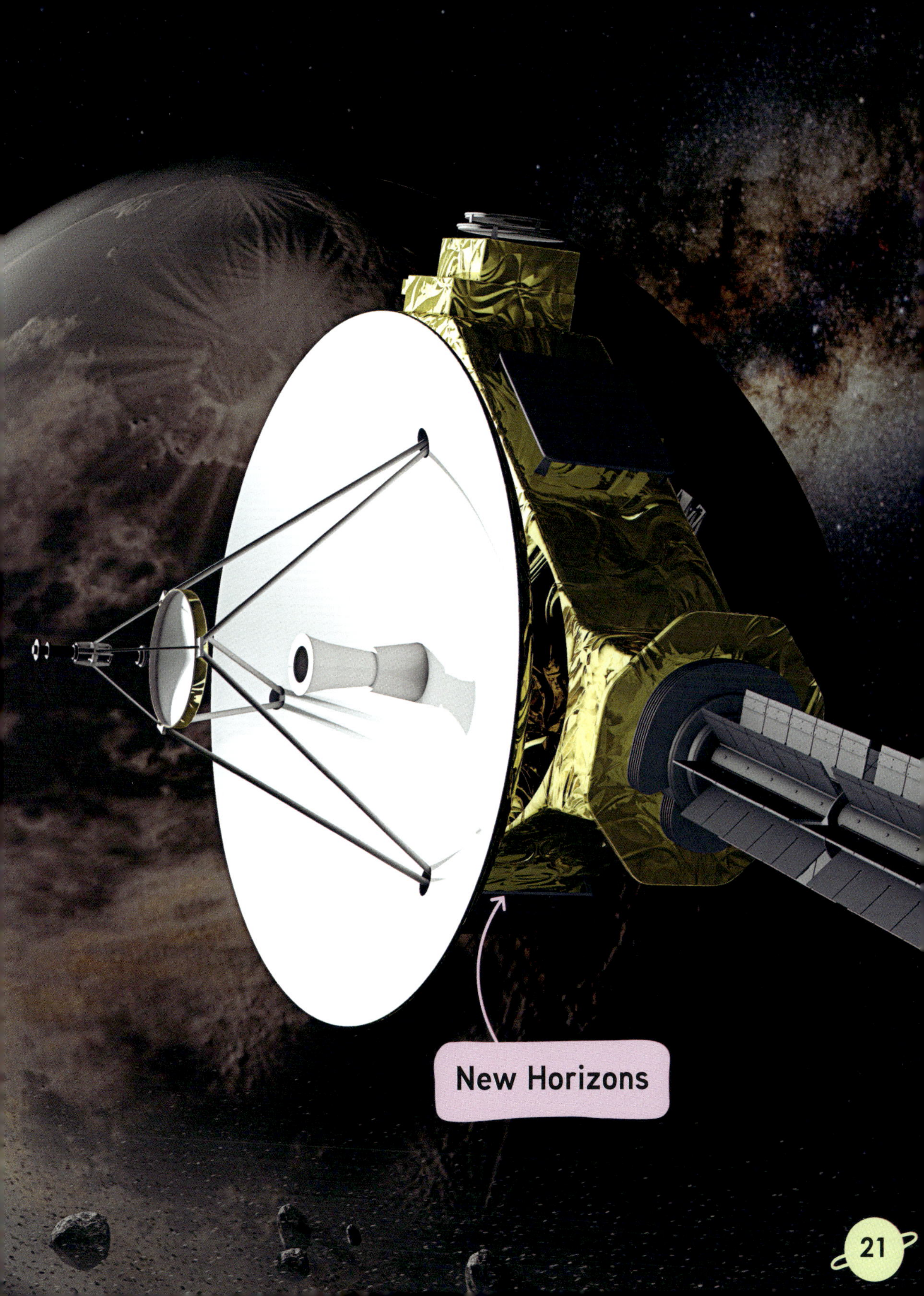
New Horizons

WHAT'S NEXT?

There is still so much to learn about Pluto, dwarf planets, and the Kuiper Belt.

Scientists want to learn about what is happening beneath Pluto's surface. They think there might be an ocean underneath!

Charon

Pluto's moon Charon has a huge **canyon** running across its entire face. Future space missions would pay a visit to discover more.

GLOSSARY

Asteroid belt – an area between Mars and Jupiter where lots of space rocks can be found.

Canyon – a deep and narrow valley with steep sides.

Decades – periods of time lasting for ten years each.

Dwarf planet – large, round objects that orbit the Sun, but aren't big enough to be called planets.

Earth years – the amount of time that a year lasts for on Earth (365 days).

Gases – substances that are neither solid nor liquid, and have no fixed shape. Many gases are invisible.

Glacier – a very large, thick block of ice.

Hubble Space Telescope – a telescope in orbit around Earth.

Kuiper Belt – a large area beyond Neptune where small, icy objects, and asteroids can be found.

Moons – large, natural objects that orbit a planet.

Mountains – rocky landforms that rise high above their surroundings.

Nitrogen – a colorless, tasteless gas.

Observatory – a building with scientific equipment used to study space.

Orbit – the path taken by one object circling around another in space.

Plains – large, flat areas of land.

Seasons – different times of the year, with different types of weather. Spring, summer, autumn, and winter are all seasons.

Solar system – the Sun and everything that moves around it.

Picture credits:
(t=top; b=bottom; m=middle; l=left; r=right):

Wikipedia: By ESO/L. Calçada - Pluto (Artist's Impression), CC BY 4.0 12bl; By ESO/L. Calçada and Nick Risinger (skysurvey.org) - http://www.eso.org/public/images/eso1142a/, CC BY 4.0 17tr; By NASA / Johns Hopkins University Applied Physics Laboratory / Southwest Research Institute - https://www.nasa.gov/mission_pages/newhorizons/images/index.html?id=371389 (see also http://photojournal.jpl.nasa.gov/catalog/PIA19966), Public Domain 14br; By NASA/Johns Hopkins University Applied Physics Laboratory/Southwest Research Institute - http://pluto.jhuapl.edu/Multimedia/Science-Photos/pics/Surface%20Diversity.jpg, Public Domain 10-11bg; By NRAO/AUI/NSF - http://www.eso.org/public/images/ann14059a/, CC BY 4.0 19ml. NASA: images-assets.nasa.gov/image/PIA19708/PIA19708~orig.jpg 11tr; images-assets.nasa.gov/image/PIA19968/PIA19968~orig.jpg 22ml; images-assets.nasa.gov/image/PIA00827/PIA00827~orig.jpg 18ml. Shutterstock: 6bl; Anterovium 16-17bg; Artisom P 12-13bg; BreizhAtao 9b; Dimazel 2-3bg; Dotted Yeti 6-7bg, 22-23bg, 24bg; Edobric 20-21bg; Iva Foto 4-5bg; NASA Images 1bg; Vadim Sadovski 8-9bg, 14-15bg; Vovan 18-19bg.